A Penny for Y ~~~~

Poems of Love and Loss
(Feelings Into Words)

by Sherrill S. Cannon

Illustrations by Kalpart

Strategic Book Publishing and Rights Co.

Review Requested:
If you loved this book, would you please provide a review at Amazon.com?
Thank You

Dedication

For
Kim C. Cannon
My Forever Love

Special acknowledgement to William Stahr,
my professor and mentor at The American University
who quietly guided and inspired me.

Thank you also to Lynn Eddy and Robert Fletcher
who made all my books possible.

My Creativity

No one understands – They think that I
Am writing of the feelings that I feel –
When really all I do is feel what I
Feel someone else would probably feel. The real
Emotions are not mine – Just sensitivity;
(Because I've felt that kind of feeling myself)
And then I try to put in poetry
The feelings that are felt by someone else.
I feel the way I'd feel if I were you
And something happened, how would I react?
The feelings, not the circumstance are true –
The intensity is mine, but not the fact.
For I rely on sensitive empathy...
And therein lies my creativity.

Acknowledgements:

Thanks to the many people in my life: students, family, friends, for allowing me to put feelings into words. As a Valentine, I have always been preoccupied with love in all its many forms, and I have also found great joy in writing poetry. As a teacher, I used poetry to help counsel many troubled teens and friends, and have continued this pattern throughout the years. *A Penny for Your Thoughts* combines all my loves into a book full of feelings.

Special mention and many memories to:
Carol, Debbee, Ellen, Francine, Gez, Joanie, Jody, Judy, Julian, Kate, Mark, Mike and many more.

And as always, thanks to my wonderful family:
KC, Christy, Kell, Steph, Kerry, John, Cailin, Paulo, Megan, John, Josh, Parker, Colby, Lindsay, Tucker, Kelsey, Mikaila, Kylie, Cristiano, Chloe, and my brother Sandy.

Special thank you to KJ of Kalpart Illustrations who have created the illustrations and book covers for all of my books including this one!

Please also consider my Award-Winning Children's Books, emphasizing consideration for others!
My Little Angel, The Golden Rule,
Mice & Spiders & Webs. . . Oh My!,
My Fingerpaint Masterpiece, Manner-Man,
Gimme-Jimmy, The Magic Word,
Peter and the Whimper-Whineys, Santa's Birthday Gift

Love & Loss: Coin Toss?

Table of Contents

HEADS . . . Of Love and Friendship

ANGEL WINGS

I send my love
On angel wings
To brush your brow
With whispered kiss...
I send my love
On angel wings
To hold you close—
Safe in my pocket
Of prayer.

A PROMISE

I promise that I shall remember

That you love me;

And never doubt,

Even though we go our separate ways

To meet again in days, months, years

Or never to meet,

That our love will always be . . .

Strong, deep, pure, and true—

A beacon light to guide us in our future

friendships;

Ever knowing that somewhere—someplace—

There is someone waiting

Who loves . . .

And remembers.

A SIGN

In the depths of my winter
I heard a small bird—
Braving the cold,
Bringing the word.
He gave my heart hope
As I heard him sing—
Three little notes
Promising spring.

A SONG

What can I give you, who's given to me
A heart and a soul and a mind that is free . . .
The love of my body? The love of my soul?
The pledge of a love that will never grow old?
The gift of a rainbow? A sweet melody?
The softness of baby? The scent of the sea?
What can I give you, to whom I belong:
The essence of love, distilled in a song.

A MOTHER BIRD'S SONG

How wonderfully she sings, how true she flies—
My little bird who suddenly has grown;
Who soon no longer calls my nest her home,
But in full plumage, migrates to new ties . . .
I raised her well, I gave her all my love;
I sheltered her and taught her all the things
To help her dare to trust her fragile wings . . .
And now I see her soaring high above.
My heart is filled with love and joyous pride
To see my little bird perform so well—
To know that she deserves her accolades.
She sings with strength and beauty deep inside—
And I will raise my voice to join the swell
Of acclamation, gratitude, and praise.

A SPECIAL PERSON

At certain times in life there comes along
A special person; who shares way deep inside
The inner spark that makes of life a song
Of love and beauty, reaching far and wide.
It does not matter what that person's age,
Nor creed nor sex nor color of the skin,
Nor size nor shape nor beauty of the face—
But just that certain something deep within
That touches and warms up a kindred heart
And kindles love; to whom you can relate—
And once more let your inner feelings start
To make you want to give and to create . . .
And I'm so very glad that I found you
To help me start to sing my song anew.

DICHOTOMY

Two hear the music:
One listens to the lyrics—
One the melody.

GOD IS LOVE

When God created man, He brought forth life—
And in His image made, we fall or stand;
For we, when standing, fall if we have strife
Within our hearts—where He has love for man.
For as He gave us life, He helps us live,
And by His will we grow to what we are;
His love for us, unchanging—ours to give,
And by and through His love, follow His star . . .
To reach the Bethlehem within our hearts,
Where lies at birth the source of joy's release:
Our comfort in new world, where God imparts
The infant Love to hearts reborn in peace;
For there in constancy—world without end,
Is love of God for man, and friend for friend.

FIRST LOVE

The me
That I was
Loves the you
That you were . . .
Old memories
Cause
My heart
To stir—
Now I find
Traces of
First love
Still there,
In the lingering
Warmth
Of a thought
And a
Prayer.

HISTORY

I do not think what might have been—
Through life, we've taken different paths.
We broke apart our hearts back then
To follow dreams we thought would last.

But now our paths have crossed once more,
It seems we've never been apart—
I knew when you walked through the door,
I'd found my missing piece of heart.

INSTRUMENTAL

Treasure all the times that we are sharing:

Open up your heart to hear my song—

From my heart, a melody of caring . . .

Rhythms asking your heart to respond.

And in tune we'll sing the deeper meanings—

Notes blending to chords of harmony—

Lyrics still unwritten, music streaming

On and on to form a symphony.

Value all the time we've spent together—

Every minute plays its special part;

Since each moment is a note forever

Harmonized within the singing heart.

Endless, let that melody remain . . .

Repeated as an ever-soft refrain.

I THINK OF YOU . . .

A glorious, lovely, sun-filled day—
I stand and watch the children play—
I think of you . . .
And my lips smile.

A crowded, dim-lit, smoke-filled room—
I sit and listen to a tune—
I think of you . . .
And my eyes smile.

A darkened, quiet, peace-filled night—
I lie in prayer, my eyes shut tight—
I think of you . . .
And my heart smiles.

LOVE THOUGHTS

If ever in a quiet moment you feel
A gentle happiness—or if a small
Sense of deep contentment seems to steal
Over your heart—you will know that all
The thoughts of love that I am sending you,
Over all the miles that we're apart,
Have crossed the distance—and are getting through
To put my special love into your heart.

I wonder if it takes a little while
For them to have to travel all that way . . .
Does it take long for them to cross the miles?
Does it take longer, the further they're away?
Or could it be whenever I think of you,
You might just then be thinking of me too?

LULLABY

Put this in your heart, and go to sleep:

That I love you with a love that grows

With every impulse causing heart to beat . . .

I love you all the beauty of a rose,

And all the droplets in a waterfall,

And all the thankful prayers that rise above . . .

I love you winter, summer, spring, and fall,

And all the poems and songs and dreams of love,

And all the special blossoms in gardens of flowers . . .

I love you with the sunlight that brings the morn,

And with the myriad stars in the darkest hours . . .

I love you with the wonder of love newborn,

And the eternal rocking swell of the boundless deep . . .

Put all this in your heart, my dear . . . and sleep.

LOVE

p
u

s
e
o
g

e
v
o
L
A
n
d

d
o
w
n -

y,

k

It reaches the s

And touches the g

r

o

u

n

d.

top,

Sometimes it's on

And sometimes

below

And SomeHOW, sometimes, it doesn't even

–   —.

up

Whether   or

down,

Oɹ ∩bꙅiqɘ qoʍu,

ro

Love is always, always, always a   u

.dn

MUSIC

Stop and hear the music in your life—
A melody for you to sing along;
For it will soothe your heart and ease your strife,
If you will only listen to its song.
You hear the children singing as they play . . .
The sounds of laughter as your friends rejoice . . .
The gentle hush and murmur when you pray . . .
The tone of love expressed within a voice . . .
They all combine in music's poetry—
A song of life embracing all your soul:
Giving all your days a harmony,
Refreshing you and helping to console—
For there is music singing everywhere . . .
If you will stop to listen, it is there.

MY BEAR

Just hold me close! Enfold me like a bear
And take me from the world into your lair:
Enveloped in your strength beyond compare;
Protected from a world that's bleak and bare.

Yet also be my tender teddy bear:
And let me trust, and tell you that I care;
Security and comfort, let us share;
And to each other, inner feelings air.

For in your arms, I know that I can dare
To face a world with no love anywhere,
Save only what I feel when you are there.

The two of us will be a gentle pair
Of lovers who have found a love so rare
That even in the darkness, it is fair.

MY SECRET SMILE

You said you love me too!
I hug it to my heart—
And every time I think of it,
A little smile will start.

It's such a happy thought—
A scene in memory
That bursts into my busy mind,
And gets a smile from me.

And people smile; they see
That twinkle in my eye—
They know that I am happy, but
They really don't know why.

I'll keep my thought within me,
To last a long, long while—
I'll hear you say, "I love you too,"
And smile my secret smile.

PEDESTALS

It must be very hard to be
The object of idolatry—
For every time you turn around,
You're off your pedestal, on
the
ground!

It's hard to stay enshrined up there—
Surrounded by a reverent air;
When in your inner heart you know
That you more truly belong
below.

So I'll not set you high above,
Revered with an adoring love—
I'd so much rather have you be
Down
to
earth, along with me

PHILOSOPHY

There is a reason for Everything,

And . . .

Everything always works out for the Best;

So . . .

Make the Best of Everything!

PROPOSAL

If you could come home to me every night
And fold me in your arms for an embrace
Of quiet strength and warmth, your eyes alight
With love for me, to show my special place ...
If you could keep your love for me aglow—
A light within your heart that shines for me,
So as the years go past your love would grow
Into a beacon of security ...
If you would let me be companion-moon,
And never let me from your orbit stray;
But, shining on my heart as sun at noon,
Let my reflections generate new rays ...
If you would be my light—my sun above ...
Then let me share your life, and give my love.

RAIN

The cold rain is falling—
The sky is wet and gray—
The birds and fragile flowers
Have all gone away . . .
A north wind is blowing—
The leaves have left the tree . . .
But I have brightest sunshine—
Because you care for me!

RECTITUDE

Great is the feeling of love
I have for you; sent from above
And blessed by God. And
No one can ever really understand
The depth of it.

Just as He sent it, and
Only as He meant it,
And interpreted by Him. And
No one can ever really understand.
I am only filled with gratitude, for an
End to my life of solitude.

SONG

My heart is so full
Of love for you, that it sings
Without any words.

REUNION

We meet again—and we are just the same.
Even though it's been a long, long while
Since we have been together, nothing's changed.
The face is etched more deeply, but the smile
Is still the same. The time that we were absent
From each other, only links the yesterdays
Of our times together, to the present—
With a span of love that joins the days.
For in reunion, that seems just a pause
In time—A brief interlude before
Resuming where we are today. Because
We are still the same. The inner core
Of love is there. And there is no more sorrow . . .
For in our lives, there will always be tomorrow.

SONNET TO FRIENDSHIP

Time will always change the way we look:

It takes away the beauty that is youth;

And never stops to question what it took,

But goes on ever marching, baring truth.

And Time will change the way we live and act:

For people judge our actions by our years;

And what did once enhance, may then detract,

For age must give up, what to youth adheres.

But Time will never change the way we are:

Our deepest inner thoughts and feelings stay;

And so a love of souls becomes a star

That shines as bright tomorrow as today.

And thus I know our love will never end . . .

For we are more than lovers—we are friends.

THAT SMILE

That sparkling smile that spreads across your face
In dawning recognition I have come;
And as it moves, extends its shining grace,
Enlightening and warming, as the sun;
And growing stronger, reaches to your eyes,
Where all at once springs forth a deeper glow,
As love and joy shine through without disguise,
From penetration to the heart below;
And then at last bursts forth in glory bright—
That dazzling smile as if the Sun did greet;
And as the moon reflects the sun at night,
My own smile mirrors happiness complete . . .
And all the world lies basking in the light
That's generated when our two smiles meet.

SPARE ME YOUR LOVE . . .

Spare me your love, if I have not
Your loyalty of heart;
For I can't bear to share a love
That's given and forgot.

Spare me your love, if I have not
Your understanding mind;
For I need more, the core of me
Is empathy of thought.

Spare me your love, if I have not
Your friendship of the soul;
For I can't then depend on you
To give me all you've got.

But if you give me all above;
The total of your heart;
Your mind and soul and whole of self—
Then, spare me not your love.

THE BOX

An old, forgotten box
With timeworn, musty locks . . .
Sitting by itself,
Up on a shelf—

Cobwebs and dust,
Tarnish and rust,
Collected with years
Of neglect and tears—

Inside, might hold
Treasures untold . . .
Somehow your inspiration
Found the right combination.

THE CROCUS

The crocus is a herald of the Spring:
Pale and shy, it lifts its tiny head,
Thrusting through the barren flower bed
To show the world that Winter's on the wing.
And as it bravely starts its flowering,
We know that though the earth seemed cold and dead
'Twas only sleeping, while the Winter fed
The tiny plant, alive yet slumbering.

So as the crocus signals the cycle anew
Of growth to fruitful harvest before the snow—
So, too, each new beginning in my heart:
Fragile crocus of Spring, with hope that love too
Will have a chance to blossom and to grow
To form a seed to last when we must part.

THE REAL ME

I have a place within me that is mine—
It holds the secret treasures of my heart;
It knows what I hold sacred and divine;
And is remote—a part of me, apart.
The deepest inner feelings of my soul—
The part of me that really is my self—
Is such a minor part of greater whole,
That very few know of its secret wealth.
But should we once become close friends, you'd see
That I am so much deeper than you deemed;
For all my best I hold inside of me,
Within myself—like treasures un-esteemed . . .
But to the ones I love, I'll give the key
To unlock all my feelings, hopes and dreams.

THE ROSE

I opened my heart
And found you there already . . .
A soft rose in bloom—
Touching my inner self
With petal fingers.

A fragile blossom
Of unfolding layered beauty . . .
My soft rose of love—
Forever blooming in my heart,
Caressing my soul.

TO A HOLLY TREE

Lovely holly tree—
Growing straight and tall,
With your prickly leaves,
Evergreen for all—
I won't be a bird
That feeds upon your boughs . . .
I won't be a squirrel
That your branches house . . .
I won't be a tree
That needs your berries bright . . .
I'll just offer love—
I'll be your sunlight

WHEN I SEE YOU AGAIN . . .

You open the door . . .
I fall into your eyes—
As your arms go around me,
And clasp my heart.

TO SEE THE FUTURE

If I could see into the future, I wouldn't—
For I don't think I'd want to know ahead
Of time, all the many things I shouldn't
Or couldn't do or be before I'm dead.
For if I knew ahead of time, then I
Would live my life according to its end;
And never give the present, time to try
To satisfy my soul. I would depend
On what I knew would happen; so I'd miss
The joys and unexpected bliss found
In present things—like getting a hug or kiss
From someone I love deeply—or the sound
Of your voice telling me you love me too . . .
Which means far more than any future view

TRUST

Put your hand in mine and come with me
Along the magic ways of love's fresh start;
  Making of your soul a bird set free,
  Waking to the music in your heart,
And singing out the wonder that you see.

Let your bird be tamed and wear a band—
  Love and give and do not be afraid . . .
And with gentle touch I'll take your hand,
Care for you with love that will not fade,
Ease your mind, and always understand.

WHAT IS BEAUTY . . .

Water lilies floating in a cool, clear pond;
Sunlight filtering on a mirrored lake;
How can my heart see, and not respond
To the beauty of design in a soft snowflake?
Dark mountains silhouetted against the dawn;
Amber sunsets in a purple-streaked sky;
The melody that lingers when the bird has gone;
How can my heart see, and not reply?
The glory of a symphony with silver and gold;
The loveliness and grace in a young dancer;
The youth still within the eyes of the very old;
How can my heart see and not answer?
Only when you care enough, is their beauty seen—
For only with love do they become what they seem.

THORNS

Where are my thorns?
I used to have many—
Sharp and pointed and prickly,
To keep anyone from
Getting too close.
I could hurt.
I could be proud—
And say nothing mattered
But my own blossom,
My own love.
But now that you are
Growing next to me—
Entwined around my life,
Sharing my soil,
And my soul—
My thorns are gone . . .
And I am soft and smooth
And terribly vulnerable
To you.
I need you.
I love you.
Where are my thorns?
They have grown velvet
With love.

WINTER'S NUPTIALS

Nature's waiting heart now sings
As she prepares to wed her king;
As she puts on with loving care
The lacy bridal gown he brings.

As through the fall he did prepare
To wed the matron cold and bare,
Transforms her to a maid again
And puts snow lilies in her hair.

And thus as it has always been,
Their sacred marriage, God attends;
The promised wedding vows to keep,
While all the world breathes the amen.

For from their union, so complete,
In consummation, earth will reap
The wonders of the seeds they sow
As on their wedding night they sleep.

And in her womb, the embryo
Of infant Spring, protected grows
Beneath the blanket of the snow . . .
The Winter's wedding gift of snow

SPINNING—Of Related Emotions

A LESSON

Look, children, see the funny clown—
His face is smiling, but his eyes are sad . . .
I think that he must be a little mad
To put on all that paint and go around
Performing tricks, and jumping up and down,
And doing silly things to make us glad—
When underneath, it seems he's feeling bad . . .
And he can't even show it with a frown.

It does no good to try to wear a mask,
And go through life pretending what you feel.
Remember, children—as emotions grow,
They need to share—so this is what I ask:
If, underneath, your heart knows what is real . . .
Why not let your inner feelings show?

A LONGING

I know I'm loved, but still I'm insecure . . .
My longing heart cries out for something more—
And I don't know just what I'm searching for,
For what it is, I'm still not very sure:
A perfect love, that's strong yet sweet and pure?
A love to make my thoughts and feelings soar?
A love that satisfies, deep in my core,
That I can trust forever to endure?
All this I have, and yet my heart still longs
For something deeper—that may never be . . .
How can my heart find out just what belongs
Within that empty space inside of me,
When even I cannot identify
The longing that still makes me want to cry?

A MEMORY

You've given me a memory to keep . . .
To hold onto whenever I am alone,
And fear and dread become a cold stone
Within my heart—causing me to weep
For all that might have been. For when that deep
Sense of loss crushes me—and unknown
Specters haunt my dreams and set a tone
Of sad regret, for I'm not ready to sleep
Yet—I'll bring my memory out, and hold
It close to me . . . Remembering the special time
You kept me safe and warm—when you gave
Me so much love, reaching out to enfold
Me in your arms and hold me close. And I'm
Sure I will remember—beyond the grave.

A POET'S PHOTOGRAPH

I take a small negative—
Enlarge it—
And my print
Makes total holocaust
Out of disappointment.

APPEARANCES

The clown with painted face and saddened eyes
Makes people laugh. The woman with the bag
Of trash clutched to her breast gets sighs
Of pity; yet even if she seems a hag
With dirt and broken fingernails, no one knows
What she thinks or how she feels. The clown
May be a way to liven up the shows,
But no one knows if he is up or down.
There is no way to see what is inside
The heart and mind of any one of us.
We see the shell and what is on the outside,
But only what we're meant to see. The fuss
Or sneers we make reveals our own crises . . .
We all have masks to provide identities.

AUTUMN

The trees are spreading
A patchwork quilt to blanket
The earth for winter.

AWAKENING

Thirsty, unaware, for still asleep . . .
Over all my heart, enchanted spell
With its power to dull, let nothing seep
Into the drought within my dusty cell.
Lost in arid dreams, I slumbered on,
Lasting till you brought me to the brink;
In your care, aware that sleep was gone
And my 'wakened heart began to drink . . .
Making all my being come alive,
Splashing me to consciousness of all;
Tasting of awareness, sense revived.
And in grateful love, I still recall
How you waked my sleeping heart to sing . . .
Renewed by potent drink of Pierian Spring.

BRIEF MEETING

It's over now—it's finished, ended, done . . .
The time that I so longed for, now has gone;
The day that took eternity to come,
Was night before I scarcely saw the dawn.
How could the time that plodded so before—
When moments seemed like ages to endure—
Pass in a flash, when you came in the door
And brought the day that did the night ensure?
For now in dragging darkness I must plan
To pass the time until you come again;
With memories of how my day began,
And how "to be" became the past "has been" . . .
The agonizing waiting through the night
Until the next brief flaring of the light.

DARK FUTURE

I see the dark clouds massing overhead—
Soon there won't be sunshine anymore:
My vital joyous world will soon be dead;
And on my bright tomorrows, rain will pour.
For now, the sun grows stronger every day—
Its incandescence permeates my core.
And yet I know that soon it'll go away,
And it will seem much darker than before . . .
I know that this is how it has to be—
That everything that starts must have an end—
But how I wish that I could stop the time,
And keep these special moments close to me—
And hold you close, my sunshine and my friend—
And leave the darkening rainclouds far behind.

DOES MEMORY LAST FOREVER?

Does memory last forever?
Does it last beyond the grave?
On the day of Resurrection
Will I know that I've been saved?

Will I remember all my loved ones?
Will I still love every one?
Will I know what I am missing—
What I've done and left undone?

Will I think of special moments
That made my life worthwhile?
If so, I'll take my memories
And go with a brave smile.

DOG AND CAT

I am the puppy dog
That wriggles all over with joy
When you approach
And likes to just be close, to look at you
And feel your nearness
And is content.

But you are the cat
That disdainfully sits on its haunches
And approaches for love when needed
And purrs and likes to be rubbed,
And then goes on his independent way
And is content.

FEAR

Ugly, black, hairy spider . . .
Hiding in the shadowed places—
Lurking in its funneled web . . .
Brushed my life, and touched my
heart with horror
As it scurried for a cover of
darkness
In the hidden recesses of myself.

FROZEN WASTELAND

I was living in a wasteland—
Where nothing new would grow,
Except to just grow older
Underneath the freezing snow.

A land of frigid icicles,
Coating the slow decay
Of a mind, that once so fertile—
Had begun to waste away.

A dreary, dismal wasteland,
Cold and barren—desolate;
Where my dreams had frozen solid,
And I was disconsolate.

There was nothing left, but aging—
Growing colder through the years ...
In a land of no tomorrows—
Only ice and frozen tears.

But you came to me and took me
From the Winter of my heart—
Where I lived before I met you,
And where nothing new could start—

To a land of youth and beauty,
Where I never shall grow old . . .
For you took my hand and led me
Into sunshine from the cold.

FLOWERS

In my spring, you came into my heart
Bringing sunny daffodils and bright
Dreams of love. And from the very start
You took my soul and turned it toward the light.
In my summer, you returned and brought
Me lilies, pure and lovely; with a promise
That in time, all our bright dreams ought
To bloom—then gave my soul your sunshine kiss.
In my fall, will there be gentle roses
Soft and intricately petalled to twine
Around our souls, as fading light closes
On our lives together—yours and mine?
And in winter, when no flowers form . . .
Will you bring me love to keep me warm?

INSIGHT

I said . . . "I'm tired of the ache;
Sometimes I wish my love could pall
And then depart."
You said . . . "But why not admit
That it can't for you won't let it?"

I said . . . "I wish that I could hate;
But I don't want to build a wall
Around my heart."
You said . . . "But aren't you aware
That there is already one there?"

IN PASSING

I can't be just a casual friend—
I love you too much to try to pretend
That you don't mean anything special to me,
A mere acquaintance is all you could be—
And I think that I would rather die
Than nod nonchalantly when you walk by.

LOST TIME

I feel the precious time slipping away . . .
Days I should be able to spend with you
Are gone—never to return. They fade
Into the past—not even any residue
Of memory to keep. Just wasted time
That's gone and will not ever come again.
With pain, I know that life will pass its prime;
I ache from sensing what there might have been.
For as the days go plodding on their way,
Relentlessly progressing one by one,
I feel the sadness lost in yesterdays
That could have been tomorrows just begun
If only I had had more time to spend
With you, my dearest love and closest friend.

GRANDFATHER CLOCK

The pendulum sways with a tick and a tock,
Relentlessly played by the grandfather clock
As it stands in the room in a place all alone,
And measures the time with its slow metronome;
With a tick and a tock as the moments pass by,
Turning minutes to hours to days as they fly
Into months and then years as the time marches on,
As the pendulum sways and continues its song
Of the tick and the tock of the grandfather clock,
Forever its fulcrum continues to rock;
Recording the things it has seen every day,
As the people grow up and then go on their way;
The time it has captured, the time that has been,
So many good times that won't happen again
As the pendulum swings with its tick and its tock,
And permanence, lastingness, seems to mock;
Turning future to present and present to past,
And what once was first will later be last
As the clock goes on beating each hour by hour,
The taste of the sweet leaves the scent of the sour;
The pendulum sweeps with a tick and a tock,
The aging heartbeat of the grandfather clock

As it swings and it sways in funereal beat,

While the time comes full circle and is complete;

And the ones that were young are now quite old,

The clock loses warmth and becomes very cold;

And the tick and the tock of the grandfather clock,

Begins to waver and finally knock

On the sides, on its walls,

In the echoing halls

Of the empty house,

Nobody to rouse;

Cold as stone;

All alone,

The clock

Stopped.

MAKING A MEMORY

I want to stop this moment in my life:
This special time that you now share with me—
And with a poet's pen or sculptor's knife,
Imprint or carve it in my memory.
I want to paint a picture in my mind—
A photograph to capture all we do—
So when I am alone, I still can find
The splendor of that time I spent with you.

I savor every second of the time—
Aware that as I spend it, it is gone . . .
Trying to remember every line
Of dialogue and actions going on—
So I can keep it always in my heart,
To replay and relive when we're apart.

MOODS

Anticipation!
Happy heart singing . . .
Love thoughts winging
Through the air!!!

    Desolation:
    Empty aching.
    For all my waiting . . .
    You're not there.

NOTHING

At first you were nothing to me—
And now you are nothing again . . .
But, oh the pain in my heart—
I know what might have been.

LOVING TIME

I long to live that loving time again
When I was all to you, and you to me . . .
That time of total giving, even when
We knew that we must part eventually.
But now that loving time has slipped away,
For what was once the present now is past;
And all the glory of that former day
Has faded in a dream that could not last . . .
For how can we recapture what was new,
When time erodes the wonder and the glow
And newer loves can offer brighter hue?
While memory pretends it does not know
That what we had was really quite unique:
A precious love that even angels seek.

MY TREE

Just outside my garden,
I found a little tree—
Growing straight and tall,
Alone, but proud and free.
The raindrops gave it water,
The sun shone from above,
The dark rich earth sustained
its roots . . .
I gave it all my love.

And now my tree is massive,
Spreading up so high—
Reaching for the rainbows,
Stretching for the sky.
I found it needed water,
And sunshine constantly—
I found it needed all the earth . . .
But did not need me.

OASIS

I wonder if you ever think of me . . .
My own cascade of thoughts make a barrage
Of flowing dreams as boundless as the sea,
And find a brief oasis in mirage.
I pass the place we met and look for you . . .
Aware you can't be there, my heart still leaps
And surges with a flood of love anew;
The empty strand remembers still the deeps:
When love made fertile, life of desert sand,
And quenched the parched soul's eternal thirst;
Refreshing streams of communication ran,
And springs of effervescent gladness burst;
Where flowers grew amid the barren waste . . .
When you gave me of love, the first taste

OLD WOMAN

Life sketches echoes of the past
Across her face: lines around her eyes
And mouth, furrows on her forehead—cast
In permanent parchment. The creases so disguise
The woman still inside, no one can see
The little child or lovely maid within.
The mind that looks on life so eagerly
Is hidden by the wrinkles of the skin.
For what is youth, but just a state of mind—
A way to look on life—to stay aware?
And who can say what love that one could find,
If one could know the person hidden there:
The youthful laughing girl who lives inside . . .
And cannot understand why she's denied

OLD AGE

I see the signs of autumn:
The leaves have turned to brown;
Some of them are hanging on,
The rest are falling down.

I know that there are new leaves
Hidden in each tree;
Waiting for the springtime birth,
The cycled destiny.

I wonder if the old ones,
Slowly letting go,
Care that they have been replaced
Or if they even know . . .

And if the ones still hanging on
Are full of silent cries—
Resenting new ones being born
For every one that dies.

PATHWAY

When I started out this morning, I didn't
know how far I'd go—
For the pathway looked inviting—where
it wound, I did not know;
And I wandered, caring nothing for the
time that passed me by—
For everything seemed bright and new,
with many things to try.

The sun was warm upon my face, the pathway
beckoned me
To follow each new winding twist—see
all that I could see.
My steps became more safe and sure—with
joy I looked about . . .
I knew that pretty soon I'd know just
why I started out.

By afternoon, the sunshine seemed to
beat upon my head—
I thought of turning backward and retracing
steps—instead
I kept on trudging forward, hoping just
around each bend
I'd glimpse what I'd been longing for—
before I reached the end . . .

Now I'm tired, oh so tired, and I cannot
understand
When this pathway, once so fertile, turned
to dusty, dried-out sand—
I know I can't go backward—I'm not
sure I'd find the way . . .
And I can't help wistful wishes I were
starting out today . . .

PETER PAN

I think that I must be part Peter Pan:
I'll grow up, but I'll not grow old nor age—
I'll live within my magic Never-land,
Where never will I reach a finished stage.
I'll keep my hopes and dreams bright, fresh, and new—
And from my deeper feelings never part:
My love for Michaels, Johns and Wendys too
Will form a Tinkerbell within my heart—
I'll try to free each Tiger Lily's mind
To find the freedom giving love enjoys;
And with my understanding, help to find
The steadfast love that's lost in the Lost Boys . . .
By staying young at heart, rob Captain Hook
Of all the youth and joy that once he took

REENTRY

Every time you come back

Into my life

My heart stops

Whatever it's doing

And leaves

With you.

PERSPECTIVE

I have climbed the mountain. I look out
On all the beauty stretching far below—
The wonder and the splendor all about
Me, as I see the things that show
From this distance. For I cannot see
The pettiness I saw as I passed through—
The insignificant things that bothered me
Before I reached this awe-inspiring view.
For now I see the panoramic sight—
The total plan, of which I saw a part
When I was on the ground—but now this height
Has shown me what's important in my heart—
And I am closer, now that I'm away . . .
For I can see the best of yesterday.

PRECEDENCE

The U.S. is stocking its arsenals,
While Russia keeps pace with its arms—
An earthquake has leveled Mexico,
And Israel's sounding alarms—
People are starving in Africa,
And also in New York, I fear . . .
But the Cowboys are beating the Redskins—
And Duke's undefeated this year.

Hundreds of children are missing—
Another airplane has crashed—
Mary's aborted her pregnancy—
It's doubtful our marriage will last—
I think that I may be dying,
But you neither hear nor care . . .
For the Dodgers are winning the Pennant—
And the Angels haven't a prayer.

READY

Death stopped by for me today—
I said I couldn't go . . .
My house was a mess, my children undressed,
And someone I loved didn't know.

Death said she'd come back later, when
I'd had more time to spend . . .
To fix my house, my family rouse,
And to give you my love, my friend.

I'll keep my house in order now,
So when death comes anew—
I can go, because I'll know
I'll have done all that I could do . . .

REDWOOD

Redwood—
Strong, solid . . .
Tallest of all—
Independent . . .
(Alone)

Roots reach
Deep—only
Earth and water—
Needs nothing else . . .
(But sun)

REQUIEM

I heard a requiem one day—
I was afraid it played for me:
The solemn faces all around
Looked not at me, but at the ground:
And in such somber company,
The mournful notes began to play—
And no one knew the words to say;
They hummed and murmured all off-key—
And in between the dismal sound,
With sobs of grief and woe, I found
That someone sang a harmony
That woke me up. I got away.

SEESAW MOODS

See-saw—
Up and down—
Touch the sky—
Hit the ground . . .
On the top—   See-saw—
Underneath—   Back and forth—
Singing joy—   Facing South—
Utter grief . . .   Back to North . . .
    Up, Spring—   See-saw—
    Down, Fall—   To and fro—
    Bitter gall . . .   Need to go . . .
    Do you—
    Do you not—
    Love me—
    Want to stop . . .

SEPARATION

The flowers are dying in their crystal vase.
They bloomed bravely for a long time
After they were cut. I put them in a place
Where they could see the sun. But now I'm
Afraid that setting and water isn't enough.
No matter how much care I give to them,
They need the plant they came from, to be tough
Enough to last; with roots, not just a stem
That's severed and can never reach the earth.
Without that contact, they've begun to die—
And sunlight and water in crystal have no worth;
For I cannot revive them, though I try.
It's sad to see such beauty go to waste . . .
Perhaps I shouldn't have cut them in such haste.

SMALL ANGEL SOUL

Small angel soul within

Myself: Talks to God

And answers prayers with

Love . . .

Listens, and sees

And comforts:

Never sleeps;

Guards and protects;

Empathizes;

Lightens and enlightens;

Sends love thoughts

Over the miles;

Understands . . . and

Longs to be Real.

SURPRISE MEETING

You do not see me yet—then I discern
The fleet impressions crossing through your mind;
As wonder, shock, amazement in their turn,
Yield slowly spreading smile that starts to shine,
And ends by dazzling with its radiance;
As joy o'ercomes displeasure that I came,
Your love transforms your total countenance,
Expressing happiness you can't restrain.
And then your arms reach out as if to hold,
Inviting and compelling love's embrace;
And I rush in, your mirror, to enfold,
To feel your warmth—to touch again your face . . .
But this is just a dream—a fantasy;
Imagining your love, my ecstasy.

STORM

Cloudy skies portend the storm that's breaking;
All the air is charged, the winds increase;
Rolling thunder sounds; the heart is shaking,
Overcome by lightning's sharp release.
Love at last transmutes the storm to fairness,
Silently the raindrops cease to fall;
In the quiet hush, a deep awareness
Sensing love has burst the final wall . . .
Then I'll come to pray the sunshine start;
Offering you the rainbow in my heart.

TENTATIVE

Tiny, new tendril

Reaching softly . . .

Soil or

Rock?

Tendril or

Tentacle?

THAT TIME OF LOVE

That time of love will never come again . . .
When love was bright and new, and life was born;
And minutes, precious jewels to adorn
The crown of days that sparkled with the gems
Of moments that with you, I lived to spend;
And in the spending, safely saved and stored
As golden memories that heart could hoard,
And deep within my treasure chest attend.
And yet I can't forget when they were bright—
And not just antique jewels, rich and rare
That gleam in polished luster from their wear;
But shining with that incandescent light,
With which they glistened when our love was new . . .
And they reflected light that came from you.

THE FORK

I'm glad our pathways converged—
At least for a little while . . .
My world seemed so much brighter,
When looked at with a smile.

My sky was filled with rainbows,
The sun was all around—
I forgot about the shadows
That lengthened on the ground . . .

But now I see the fork ahead,
And dusk is drawing near . . .
I don't think I can bear the pain
When you're no longer here.

THE HEART

The heart is a strange and lonely thing:

It independently goes its way;

And will not listen to anything—

What people do or what people say;

Whether its loving is returned;

Whether its loving is worthwhile;

If it's accepted, or if it's spurned—

It still maintains its wistful smile

And feels the way it wants to feel,

No matter what the mind avers—

What mind denies, the heart reveals . . .

For whenever it hears your name, it stirs.

THE MAPLE

Tasting Spring, the Maple puts out buds—
Responding to the warmth within the sun,
And softening of the soil at its feet—
To open itself to another new beginning . . .
Bravely becoming vulnerable again.
The Oak, however, shows a cold reserve—
Keeping itself restrained, aloof and bare;
Not exposing its tender shoots too soon—
Knowing that an unexpected frost
Might stunt whatever delicate growth was there . . .
I wish my Maple heart were made of Oak.

THE ROAD

I do not want to leave, but I must go—
The road of life is leading me away;
And I must travel onward, even though
My longing heart is asking me to stay.
I'll bravely set my course to journey on—
Regretfully I'll say my fond good-byes;
And then set out, to do what must be done
To try to grow new roots and form new ties:
I'll follow each new road wherever it leads,
And make another home whenever it ends;
I'll find new ways to meet my family's needs,
And know that on the way I'll make new friends . . .
But from the ones I love, I'll never part—
For I will take them with me in my heart.

THE TRANSPLANT

It really wasn't very long ago,

My plant was set into this strange new ground

Where everything was different. But it found

That even in new sunlight, it could grow

And form new roots. And as it reached below

The surface, it discovered in this new compound,

Enriching nourishment that was so profound

That now its roots do not want to let go.

How did they grow so fast? These roots that cling

So tightly underneath, hardly had time

To form. How did they get to be so deep?

It must be that they found a source of Spring

That vitalized and strengthened them. And I'm

Afraid that when I pull them up, I'll weep.

THOUGHT WAVES

Think of me, and know I'm thinking too:
Over all the miles that we're apart,
Mental waves transmitted straight to you . . .
Images I send you from my heart.
Know each time you think of me, I'm there—
Even though my person's miles away—
As my thoughts come winging through the air,
Near to you, a part of me will stay:

Dreaming of the friendship that we shared,
Sending thoughts to make you think of me,
Acknowledging how very much I cared,
Needing you, and all that used to be . . .
Deep inside, my soul is wet with tears—
I'll see you in my thoughts throughout the years.

TO KEEP OUR LOVE . . .

Illusive dreams of permanence are cloying
The happiness we had in all we shared,
Beatitude from inner feelings bared,
And joyousness of life, through love enjoying.
Possessiveness and guilt have caused avoiding;
The closeness and the gladness are impaired;
Through vain desires, only pain ensnared;
And love, by thought of binding, self-destroying.
We must not long for what can never be;
For longing would destroy what could become
The essence of a love no ties effect.
To keep our love we have to set it free:
Relinquish thoughts of futile martyrdom;
Accept what cannot be, without regret.

UNIVERSE

My birth relies on Mother Earth's
Strong ties with Father Sky
So to be terse, the universe
Means I should search for why.

WHEN DEATH COMES FOR ME . . .

When death comes for me . . .

Will she call ahead of time,

So I can pack my bags

And be waiting . . .

Or will she drop in unannounced—

An unexpected visitor

To escort me . . .

Or will I have to call for her,

So that I can get away

Unattended . . .

Or—perhaps—will she just arrive

When I have gone to sleep—

And cover me . . .

WINDOWS

Life goes by in a slow blur . . .
An opaque tapestry of images
Veiled by time;
With occasional glimpses,
As windows in the clouds,
Of what might have been . . .

WINTER ARRIVES

The north wind came through,
Took down the tree ornaments,
And packed them for spring.

WINTER BRIDE

Winter wooed my tree—
Put snow lilies in her hair
And dressed her in lace

WINTER STORM

The tempest buffeted me from side to side
And back and forth, as icy gusts would blow
And rock me from my feelings deep inside;
As unprotected branches bowed below
The gales of sleet and blindly driven snow
To weight me down and bend my frozen pride,
Until there seemed to be no place I could go
And nowhere from its raging could I hide.
The Winter of my heart was bleak and bare.
Strong winds of feeling blew throughout my soul;
The cold and freezing rain was everywhere,
And nothing seemed to make my spirit whole . . .
And then came Spring: when sensing love's fresh start,
A soft breeze came along and touched my heart.

RECONNECTION

I want to make the moment last forever -
The instant when I reunite with you;
The part of me that distance could not sever
Fitting back into the space it knew.
Finding in your arms what I was missing,
Wrapped within your warmth, my heart can hide -
Realizing what I had been wishing
In my lonely heart way deep inside.
For as I find the part of me apart,
The empty aching feeling goes away;
And I find once again I have a heart
That reconnects tomorrow with today -
And I no longer live in fading past,
For I now know that love is going to last.

WORDS

Words, words, words, words—
Fill my mind like a flock of birds:
Flying, dipping, soaring, twirling,
Keeping my mind always whirling;
Singing, chirping in my heart,
Helping all my feelings start.
Bound within my heart they rage—
Gliding, diving in a cage;
Winging, darting everywhere,
For there is no way to share.
Until, finally, my heart is loosed . . .
I put them on a page to roost.

TAILS . . . of Heartache and Anguish

ALL THAT'S LEFT . . .

Where are you? I can feel you near—
But not near enough to really know
If you are here. Do I only hear
A whisper of the voice that once was so
Dominant—sounding through my soul?
Do I only see a shadow of the one
Who once had absolute and full control
Of all my feelings—my warm life-giving Sun?
I cannot find you. You are lost to me—
Going where my love can't follow you . . .
Slipping away in unreality
To a place where dreams cannot come true.
A shadow and a whisper—all that's left
Of one who was my life—and I'm bereft.

ANGUISH

Please, don't ever love me—I don't want
  your love.
Because no one could ever love me
In the way I want to be loved:
Completely ...
    intensely ...
       loyally ...
          devoutly.
My love is the only love constant.
  Don't love—
I don't want to die inside again.

Please, somebody, love me—I need someone's
  love.
There must be someone to love me
In the way I want to be loved:
Completely ...
    intensely ...
       loyally ...
          devoutly.
Is there no other love that's constant?
  Oh please—
I need to live inside again.

A SMALL DEATH

It's very cold and very dark—
A chill is on my trembling heart
Because I know I must depart.
I'm so afraid, for I must start
To find another life away
From all that means so much today—
I know there is no other way . . .
I want to stay. I want to stay.

I feel alone and so afraid
Of leaving friends that I have made
To go from sunshine into shade—
I fear that love will start to fade.
And though I haven't gone as yet—
Of all the loved ones I have met,
I ask my heart with sad regret . . .
Will they forget? Will they forget?

The freezing cold envelops me—
I have no warm security
That what I had will ever be
Found again entirely.
There is no sun, no warming ray
To touch and take the cold away—
There's only darkness when I pray . . .
Please let me stay. Please let me stay.

I am so cold and so alone—
I feel my hope turn into stone—
Once more I face the dark unknown—
I have to leave what I have known.
I weep inside—my soul is wet
And cold with dread and deep regret—
I cry, but no one answers yet . . .
Will you forget? Will you forget?

A STONE

Today I do not feel. Nothing moves
My heart. I have become a cold stone
That does not care to come alive, nor choose
To share anything. I stay hard and alone,
Completely deaf and dumb. I need no one
To try to give my granite heart a nudge;
For all it felt is over, finished, done—
And it will not be moved—it will not budge
At all. For it will never come alive
Again. The joy and gladness it received
From you is dead, and nothing can revive
Its singing life. It would never have believed,
While yesterday it sang its joyous song,
That today—forever—all music would be gone.

DEATH SENTENCE

If I were told that I was going to die
And only had a short time left to live—
You'd stay beside me, hold my hand, so I
Would have the love and comfort you could give.
You'd try to fill my heart with so much love
There wouldn't be much room for doubt and fear—
And all the dreams that I'd been dreaming of,
You'd help condense into a single year.
You'd tell me that you love me, hold me tight—
Whenever I was lonely, let me call—
You'd give me hugs, come see me through the day—
And hold me very close throughout the night . . .
I think perhaps I'm dying after all—
For I was told that I would live today.

DEJECTION

In the spring, my love was born;
It warmed my heart, and gave it light—
Yet like the sun that brings the morn,
It slowly faded into night . . .

As seasons change and years go by,
We leave our loves along the way—
The brilliant summers swiftly fly
Into the fall I live today . . .

My warm heart feels the chill advance
As autumn turns to winter cold . . .
For there will be no second chance
To keep my heart from growing old.

DISCOVERY

Creeping softly, so I couldn't see—
A little part of you crept into me.
Resting, hiding deep within my core—
Ripening and growing more and more . . .
I only found out when we had to part—
Every day the hole hurts in my heart.

A YEAR

June
Blows her
Arid breath
On July
And smothers
August.

September
Opens her
Sleeping eyes
And awakens
October

November
Spreads her
Barren arms
And embraces
December.

January
Puts her
Cold hands
On February

And stunts
March.

April
Hangs her
Willow tresses
And drowns
May.

DEPARTURE

You said the time had come for your departing;
You called good-bye to all the friends you'd met;
You smiled and waved your hand—my vision misted;
Then turned and walked away, your future starting.

And all your friends were saddened by your leaving;
They kept their cheerful faces till you'd left;
Then all at once the happiness was missing;
The stillness was the silent sound of grieving.

The younger ones were showing signs of crying;
The older—simply smiles of fond regret;
And someone asked if I were going to miss you . . .
I smiled and kept my mask, while I was dying.

EXISTENCE

Nothing seems to matter anymore . . .

My love of life has disappeared somehow;

And all the memories of times before

Bring only ache that they are over now.

The emptiness so deep and vast, compared

To all the joyousness I felt with you;

When all my thoughts and feelings could be shared,

But now there's nothing to look forward to.

My past brings ache—recalling feelings lost;

My present, just a void wherein I grope;

No future—for in sacrifice the cost

Of loving you was paid by death of hope . . .

I only know I go from day to day

Not living—just enduring time away.

FALL

The geese are flying South again—

Their sad haunting cries

Echo in my heart . . .

Spring is lost,

And bitter

WintEr

WiN

S.

FOREVER IS . . .

In my past, my equator—

Present, my horizon—

Future, abyss . . .

FOREVER LOVE

I held forever in my outstretched hands
And watched it sit upon my fingertips:
A lovely butterfly with golden bands
Of color on its trembling wings—a kiss
Of love entrusted to my longing heart.
And yet it would not stay—My forever
Left before I captured any part
Of it—It slipped away. And I will never
Know the joy I might have known if I
Had left it on its own to freely give
Itself to me—Had not had to try
To keep it to myself—Had let it live
And thrive . . . To brush my hand with gossamer
Wings that, like my heart, were still aflutter.

GRIEF

I saw a willow,

Hiding its face in its hands . . .

Silently weeping.

I SEE

The day I so looked forward to is done—
It ended before it even got its start.
And all the joy and gladness in my heart,
Was gone before it ever had begun.

The day that meant so very much to me—
The time my eager heart looked forward to—
Was not remembered nor thought of by you;
And so it never even came to be.

The special time that I anticipated—
The thought of which sang in me all the time—
Had never even entered your busy mind . . .
It was forgotten—this day I so awaited.

And now my disappointment is so deep
And vast; because it meant so much to me—
Yet meant nothing at all to you, I see.
I hang my head with opened eyes . . . and weep.

MY HEART

I sent you my heart in a package
Wrapped in brown paper and twine;
And hoped that when you received it,
Your heart would be glad to have mine.

How total was my desolation
To find out that you didn't care . . .
(It died in its box—unopened—
For you forgot it was there . . .)

LOVE'S SEASONS

In Spring, the gentle fingers of the rain
Caressed my soul and nurtured love's new start;
When first your loving hand on mine had lain,
And touched the trembling bird within my heart.
Then Summer sun, with warm and sensuous rays
Did bask my soul within its radiant heat;
My wakened bird sang melodies of praise,
When nourished by your beams of love complete.
Yet in the Fall, the moon's reflected light
Waxed shimmers on my soul, before it waned;
And bird in silvered darkness could not sing.
Now—watching Winter stars, remote, at night . . .
My wonder at the beauty has remained—
But bird has flown away to seek new Spring.

MIGRATION

I think I flew further north than I
Meant to. Everything is strange and cold.
Even the trees are different—and the sky
Is not the same. Is it that I've grown old?
And cannot adjust to change the way I did
When I was young and life stretched far ahead
Of me—When each new nest was a new bid
For me to start anew? It seems, instead,
I wish I could find my way back to my old nest
In my familiar trees—with warm skies
And the sunshine life that was the best
That I ever knew. But I didn't realize
At the time, that I'd never find my way
Back again to my ideal nest of yesterday.

MOVING AWAY

All the people in my life who've meant
So much to me, other than my family,
Are slowly fading away. The times spent
And shared with them are becoming only memories.
And although I'm happy to have had the time I had
With them—and I'm glad there's so much to remember—
I can't help feeling somewhat depressed and sad
That all my bright and flaming loves are only embers
That glow within my heart—but no longer give
The burning, searing heat that so inspires
My soul—and makes me really want to live,
And give back all the light and warmth in the fires
Of my heart. For close contact needs more than a visit . . .
And an ember isn't as glorious as a fire, is it?

MY FLOWER

My flower is dying.
It was so beautiful
When you gave it to me—
So bright
And full of the promise
Of lasting blooms.
I tried to do my best for it—
I gave it so much love . . .
I even talked to it.
But now I see it wilting—
Shriveling up and drawing away,
And there seems to be nothing
I can do . . .
I think I did too much—
I killed it
With love.

ON LOVE

You meet—and love is born:

Not with the clash of cymbals,
Nor with the sound of trumpets;
But slowly,
    quietly,
        hopefully.

Love grows—

By leaps and bounds
From one to another.
Each one's heart racing on,
One always outdistancing the other,
To love more,
    feel more,
        demand more.

Love dies;

Not with the clash of cymbals,
Nor with the sound of trumpets;
But slowly,
    quietly,
        hopelessly.

PAIN

I saw you today—
You smiled to me . . .
My throat closed up,
I could hardly see
For the tears in my eyes
As you passed me by
With a nod of your head
And a casual "Hi" . . .
For I longed to stop
And talk to you,
But that is what
I must not do.

PARADOX

In your times of pain, anguish, or need to let go,
Your beloved one has always been there;
To comfort your torment and ease your distress,
Knowing how to release you, to share.

But disconsolate pain and anguish is born
When the one that you love draws away;
For you want to share, but the one that you need
Is the one who has caused your dismay.

And the ultimate pain and anguish occurs
When the one that you love will not heed;
So you need to share, more than ever before; but—
If you could, then there wouldn't be need.

RAIN

Angry rain

Lashing at my window pane

Searching for entry

Making water webs on screens

Surf-sounding wind-driven splashes

On my transparent barrier—Screams

Of pain.

REDBUD TREE

In springtime the redbud tree bends
in the wind,
Bowing to external force—
Resilient, compliant, flexing its
branches—
Complaisant, not fighting the source.

In winter, when ice encases its bark,
And freezes its branches in place—
A turbulent wind can snap every limb,
And leave behind nothing but space . . .

ROCK

I am a rock.

I no longer care, nor feel.

I can support anything;

And I can be everything

For myself;

All by myself . . .

Alone . . .

I lie.

SACRIFICE

You didn't want to see me, yet I came . . .
The burning need within me urging on
To see if you were right and I was wrong,
And that my love for you was just a flame;
Or if I only played another game,
In which you were the king and I the pawn
To checkmate love, that flared and then was gone:
And smothered dreams of fires was to blame.
And so I came to see you in the night;
But fate, the stoker, kindled thought to see
That if I really loved you, I would go.
So I, through sacrifice, learned I was right:
Because I loved, I gave—and set you free . . .
The holocaust it caused, you'll never know.

SAND

Tiny grain of sand

Whipped by an uncaring wind

Into my frozen eye

Causing tears of pain

Melting feeling

Crying into the void

Of time

SHORT STORY

You could care—so detect it—
Your heart holds empathy . . .
And oh the hope I have inside
From dreaming of what might be.

You are giving—so protect it—
You've shared your thoughts and pain . . .
And oh the love I have inside
From sensing of what has been.

You're withdrawing—so expect it—
You won't take love from me . . .
And oh the hurt I have inside
From thinking of what should be.

You are gone—so accept it—
You'll never love again . . .
But oh the ache I have inside
From knowing what might have been.

SOMEDAY

Someday—when everyone has gone and I'm
Alone in my world—When cobwebs form across
My mind, and eyes grow dim with age—and time
Passes slowly through the shadows—My loss
Will be the deeper for the many things
I left undone along the changing ways:
The wasted search for what tomorrow brings,
While in my quest for future, lost todays—
And all I should have done and said and been
Will be recorded in the time elapsed—
What could have been will be forever gone:
For what I see now, I could not see then . . .
All my bright tomorrows turned to past,
While I was searching for another dawn.

YESTERDAY

Why couldn't this be yesterday—
When everything was fine,
And life stretched out in front of me—
A smooth, unbroken line?
I knew there'd be some snags to find,
Some snarls here and there—
But I was sure that I could cope
As long as I could share.
Today I find my life has changed,
My line has angled down—
And I'm not sure of anything . . .
For you won't be around.

THE BID

The cards were dealt, and I recipient
Of highest honors, held them in my heart;
For winning of the Master Tournament
Could mean a membership of life apart;
And bidding for the contract of our suit,
Might show our tricks to our society . . .
Our trump of hearts must be forever mute;
For thus what might have been, can never be.
I held the cards and visualized the game
That by finesse could possibly have won,
And brought to me the glory of your name
In partnership—yet your success undone . . .
So I who could have bid to make the slam—
For love of you, I passed—threw in my hand.

TIME PASSES

Time passes slowly. Every second
Beats as a steady metronome
In funereal tempo—Remorseless—To reckon
Every minute—Turning heart to stone
And memory to ashes. Dulled with dust
Of dreams that sparkled once—To fade
In tattered remnants—Shining armors rust
Within dank sunshine that has turned to shade.
And all my wishful longing will not bring
Back to me the time that now is spent
And faded into far-off hints of Spring—
When I was young and happy and content,
And time went tripping quickly, and dreams were new—
When I could spend my precious time with you.

... TO SHARE MY TEARS

When I left, it was raining everywhere.
The sky was gray and overcast. There was no
Light at all—no sunshine anywhere,
And no hope nor any sign of any rainbow.
My heart was raining inside—sad and wet
With tears it could not shed until too late
To share with you. And now I can't forget
The storm that later on would not abate—
That flooded my world with torrential lonely tears,
Because there was no shelter. And I regret
That when I was with you, I chose to wait
To be alone to weep. For my heart fears
There'll never be a chance to show—or let
You know, that never again would I hesitate ...

WALL

I bravely hold my chin up in the air,
Pretending that I don't depend on you—
That if you do not want me, I don't care,
For I have lots of other things to do.
You cannot see the pain I have inside—
The aching lonely tears within my heart—
Because I've built my wall and kept my pride,
And do not let you see me torn apart.
You think that I am happy, for I smile
And tell you that I'm busy anyway—
So you are free to live your own life, while
My heart is breaking, wanting you to say
That all you need and want in life is me . . .
Oh how I wish that I could let you see.

WINTER

The days plod on in winter shades of gray,
Like bleak and leaden skies portending snow;
My heart is numb, for hope has gone away;
I do not feel—I do not want to know.
The Spring that caused my heart to come alive,
Passed on to Summer, causing life to soar;
But then the Fall when love began to die,
Brought Winter when the ice encased my core.
I do not think—I know I do not care
To stoke the frozen ashes of my heart;
For though my life is cold and bleak and bare,
A thaw would cause myself to melt apart.
I do not want to think of anything . . .
Since there will never be another Spring.

YESTER-DAY

Yesterday my life was warm and sunny—
Happiness and joy were all around—
Everything I heard, I thought was funny,
The laughter in my heart did so abound.
I ran and shouted all throughout the day—
Exuberance and Springtime, all were mine—
My worries and my cares went out to play;
And I was young and free, and felt so fine.
The flowers in my world burst into bloom—
The spring-green trees waved their arms at me—
I sang out loud a gay and happy tune,
Exalting in my Springtime ecstasy.
Yet now, today, nothing blooms or grows . . .
My heart awoke to cold and bitter snows.

CPSIA information can be obtained
at www.ICGtesting.com
Printed in the USA
BVHW01s1248041217
501910BV00003B/523/P